"The 7 Universal Laws of Sales Success"

Ian Stephens

4th Edition – Updated August 2014

Illustrations by Peter Petrovic

Intertype Publishing

MELBOURNE, AUSTRALIA

4th Edition published in 2014 by

Intertype
Unit 45, 125 Highbury Road
BURWOOD VIC 3125 Australia

National Library of Australia Cataloguing-in-Publication entry:

Author:	Stephens, Ian
Title:	The 7 Universal Laws of Sales Success
ISBN:	978-0-9874466-3-3
Subjects:	Selling.
	Success.
	Sales management.
	Successful people.
Dewey Number:	658.8

Printed in Australia by Intertype

Graphic Design by Intertype.

Illustrations by Peter Petrovic

Disclaimer:
The material in this publication is of the nature of general comment only and does not represent professional advice. It is not intended to provide specific guidance for particular circumstances and it should not be relied on as the basis for any decision to take action or not take action on any matter, which it covers. Readers should obtain professional advice where appropriate, before making any such decision. To the maximum extent permitted by law, the author and the publisher disclaim all responsibility and liability to any person, arising directly or indirectly from any person tacking or not tacking action based on the information in this publication.

Dedicated to my wife Karina; for her love, support, encouragement, and for allowing me to be who I really am.
To Rebecca and Jay; for the love and joy they bring to our lives.

About the author

Ask Ian to share a little about himself, and he will joke that he was born cold, wet, bald, and hungry, and then things got worse!

In reality, Ian Stephens is amongst Australia's leading sales specialist and peak performance coach. Since 2006, he has been regularly listed by professional Speakers Bureau's in the top 20 business motivational speakers in Australia. He has a passion for the practical, coupled with an ability to inspire and equip people with simple everyday tools they can apply immediately to make more sales and profit.

Ian has global experience working with a large range of national and international clients, including companies such as CHEP, Brambles, Sensis (formerly Yellow Pages), World Directories (Europe), The Wesfarmers Group, Cleanaway, Smorgon Group, Redken, TAL and Australian Paper (Nippon Paper).

Prior to his years as a management consultant, speaker and facilitator, Ian progressed up the corporate ladder at remarkable speed. With practical experience in the sales world, Ian was appointed State Manager of a multi-million dollar business at the age of 24, and has managed large sales teams.

Today, Ian is in constant demand and is booked to speak/facilitate for 160 days a year. His excellent people skills not only assist companies and individuals to build and implement practical sales tools, but also to minimise the resistance associated with adopting new ways of working.

He is a co-author of The 7 Step Pathway to Mastery and the author of NOW-Powered Customer-Service, which showcases the 7 Immutable Laws of Serving Others

CONTENTS

CHAPTER ONE

INTRODUCTION

' The Seven Universal Laws of Sales Success' is written for all those who want to become or remain a Tall Poppy in the sales profession. If you want to be head and shoulders above the rest and stay there, in an industry that is one of the most demanding available, then the laws themselves are critical to your success. They apply regardless of the industry, the channel of distribution, or the product or service you sell.

I wrote this book to summarise the simple, natural and universal 'Sales Effectiveness Success' principles. It will only be of interest to you if:

1. You want to learn the seven underpinning principles of Sales Productivity.

2. You are interested in understanding a simple system that, if followed, will assist you to become (or remain) the potential Tall Poppy salesperson.

3. You want to know what makes the crucial difference between someone who can write his or her own cheque when it comes to earning potential, versus someone who just manages to survive.

Maybe as you read this introduction, you're pondering whether this is just another book of sales success secrets, with no practical application to your world?

Can I, at this point, encourage you to keep an open mind? I am absolutely convinced that in today's rapidly changing technological world, the most expensive thing you can own is a closed mind. Could I suggest you avoid making any judgments until you have digested the content, tested the principles, and seen the results you get by harnessing these natural universal laws. Tune into the wavelength of this book. Grab these tips and tools and put them to work in your sales career. Then, sit back and see the practical application in your sales life. Not to mention the increase in your sales results!

It is a book written for those experienced sales people who are looking to work smarter, and take their results to the next level. In fact, I challenge those who have played in this profession for many years to reflect on your experience, and join the thousands of seasoned Tall Poppy Salespeople who have e-mailed me, cornered me during seminar breaks, and shared their sales stories. They confirm these universal laws are as real as night and day!

To those of you new to the selling profession, I say that I wish a book containing these truths had crossed my path early in my sales career. Why? Because I could have avoided some stressful periods when there was too much month left at the end of the money!

Learn from other people's experience

I once listened to a speaker named James Rohn. One of the many pearls of his wisdom related to how we can learn. He made the assertion that one of the most effective ways to fast-track awesome results, is to learn from other people's experiences! I have travelled the world collecting stories, sharing and gathering, listening and observing, testing and re-confirming the robustness of the laws. In fact, as I sit here in August 2014 updating this edition and getting it ready for its 4th print run, I have done a rough calculation; my work in this field has taken me to 28 counties, and I have clocked up over 8,000 hours specializing in sales-force effectiveness. I have seen hundreds of people apply these laws to their field of endeavour, and witnessed the evidence of the results they have achieved. I have watched sales representatives use these laws to further their careers. I have worked hard to capture the essence of 'selling effectiveness'. I cannot count the number of times people from all walks of life within the global profession of selling have provided yet another practical example of how these laws operate and work. Why not tap into that collective wisdom? Benefit from 'other people's experience' so you can achieve better results, and avoid making the same mistakes many of us have made. Use their lessons and 'pearls' to stay away from the pitfalls which regularly trap even the most seasoned sales performers. Success leaves clues!

'Effective' versus 'efficient'

Step into the home office of my folk's house in suburban Perth, Western Australia, and you will find many sayings pinned to various corkboards; some serious, some profound, most of them humorous. One of the more serious reads…

"Efficiency is doing things right.

Effectiveness is doing the right things efficiently."

This sounds profound when you first read it, and yet, when you think it through, it is a complex statement. My wife puts it a simpler way: Doing the right things the right way!

Effectiveness and efficiency are important factors and in my various training modules and programs, I try to distinguish between the two.

In a sales context, efficiency to me is about the skill of the sales call or visit. It is about how efficiently you can build rapport, ask questions, gently guide the prospective client to realize they have needs, issues and challenges, and that your product or service solves them. It is about how efficient you are at handling the objections, which sometimes occur, and how skilled you are at closing the sale. It's all about being efficient once you are in front of the client or prospective clients.

Effectiveness is a completely different matter. To be effective in the sales world is more to do with how you spend your time, where you concentrate your energy, who you see, and for how long. And it's more than just plain old territory management. It's about acknowledging how little time there is to do the selling activity, which creates the revenue result, and playing where you will have the best results, in minimum time.

Just to manage your expectations, you won't find tips and suggestions about 'skills' and 'efficiency' in this book. I still have to finish that one. I have started mind you. The page numbers are done... I just need to fill in the content!

This read is purely about 'sales effectiveness' – a different and yet more important beast. It has taken me years to realize it, but to master the competencies associated with selling, is of little use, if you do not abide by the universal laws. Show me the very best in the world at selling, and yet, someone who at the same time abuses these 'effectiveness laws', and I will show you someone who is spinning their wheels and achieving poorer results than is possible.

No. This book is just about the...

Timeless laws of sales effectiveness

There is nothing new in the profession of selling, and I won't claim to give you anything new – just enlightenment. This industry has been around ever since Eve influenced Adam to taste that infamous apple. The effectiveness principles and tools, which guarantee success in sales, have been known for centuries. They are timeless and universal. Perhaps you just haven't been exposed to them in a way where they jump up from your subconscious mind and become conscious. They are the prod; the "wake-up call" to avoid a sales slump.

Regardless of the products and services you sell, the channels of sales and marketing you employ, or the market segment you target, they'll cut through the layers of information, which bombard your five senses every day. Be amazed as you find yourself nodding and agreeing with the laws when we cover them.

I tell people they are as real as the Law of Gravity and they relate to this analogy. Whilst it cannot be seen, gravity is there. We know, we accept without query that if you drop this book from any height, it will fall.

These "Seven Universal Laws of Sales Success"© are the same. You can't see them, but they do exist. Harness them, acknowledge them, treat them with respect and reap the rewards. Be amazed at the ease in which you produce powerful sales results. Or go with the alternative: ignore them, bypass them, side-step them or avoid them if you wish. But guess what? They are still real. They still exist, and just like gravity, they're now actively working against you, and you will suffer the consequences.

The power of a story

This book has been written as a story. Why? Because stories create magic by bringing the point to life. It also allows you, the reader, to focus on the learning and relate it to your circumstances.

A learning methodology that works

The method of delivering the principles contained in this story is referred to as the Memory Anchor Retention System ©. An easy recall tool, the methodology of learning was created by the late Roger Anthony (deceased) of Crocodiles not Waterlilies' fame. It enables the reader to remember what has been read, to recall the principles without redress to the book, and to apply them, under pressure, out there in the Jungle of Life. It tags the memory.

It is an accelerated learning process that caters to the three main learning senses: visual, auditory and kinesthetic. For those who have a preference to learn through their visual sense, you will appreciate the icons which represent each of the seven laws. They will paint a picture which clearly shows you the way forward in sales. Those who learn more effectively when their auditory sense (hearing) is stimulated will tune into the names of the laws; each is designed to prompt recall of the detail. And for those who learn best by playing with the concepts (hands-on approach), the various activities in the book will assist in the process of bringing it all together for you. You will appreciate the 'Let's get practical' section at the end of each law.

Regardless of the sensory preference, which best suits, your learning style, the aim is to ensure you can recall the laws. They should pop up from your subconscious mind when you need them most. They will then become an automatic response. My philosophy on learning and development is very simple: if you can't recall something, then how the hell can you apply it in your daily life? It is what we do on a daily basis that forms our subconscious habits, and our habits produce results – both positive and negative.

Living these laws begins with being able to instantly recall them.

My wish is that you live these laws on a daily basis, and achieve the very best results you can.

Keep It Simple, Stupid!

Dad taught me the KISS principle over dinner one night at the local Chinese restaurant. Keep it simple, stupid! The laws explored in this book are simple. They are common sense and yet, in my years of speaking, training and coaching sales professionals, I have found that common sense is not all that common. There seems to be an enormous gap between knowing and doing and I suspect the reason is because we make it too complicated.

Our mistake is we have wanted to improve on simplicity. I am reminded of the story of an old Indian chief who sat in his hut on the reservation, smoking a ceremonial pipe and eyeing two U.S. government officials sent to interview him.

"Chief Two Eagles" asked one official, "You have observed the white man for 90 years. You've seen his wars and his technological advances. You've seen his progress, and the damage he's done."

The chief nodded in agreement.

The official continued, "Considering all these events, in your opinion, where did the white man go wrong?"

The chief stared at the government officials for over a minute and then calmly replied, "When white man found the land, Indians were running it. No taxes, no debt, plenty buffalo, plenty beaver. Indian people spent all day hunting, gathering and fishing, all night having sex."

Then the chief leaned back and smiled, "Only white man dumb enough to think he could improve a system like that."

I'm not dumb enough to think I can improve on the basics but I'm sure I can clarify them. Your awareness will result in instant recognition of the path of action required.

This is not an exhaustive guide to the profession of selling and yet, when you grasp the simplicity of the laws, I know you will be eager to make them a part of your daily life. The thousands of people who have provided feedback after attending my 'Activate Your Sales Effectiveness' workshop can't be wrong. They recognise the 'productivity' application of the principles, and the 'universal truth' nature of the laws. I know you will too.

Special Bonus Material

If you would like more information on the strategies, tools and techniques available to help you improve your sales performance and grow your business register at:

www.ianstephensspeaks.com

CHAPTER TWO

The "Made two order" Induction training process…

It was a nervous and anxious Todd who commenced his first day at 'Matthews & Stephens'. He had heard a lot about the company and its approach to selling. On his third application, he had been successful in landing a role as a Territory Manager.

Todd had been welcomed by the receptionist and shown through to the Sales Manager's office. "She won't be long," she had said, "She's just been planting a few seeds!"

"Planting a few seeds;" thought Todd, "Sounds interesting!"

Before long, a professionally dressed lady walked into the office and re-introduced herself as Karina. She had a presence about her that instantly reminded Todd this lady was both successful, and comfortable with her identity and environment. "We met during the recruitment interviews. Welcome aboard, Todd. Let me show you around the building, let you get a feel for the place and then you can listen to how we do things here at Matthews and Stephens, or M&S as we refer to her."

Todd completed a tour of the office. He had soon met the entire team and was picking up on a very uncommon yet positive vibe about the place.

Returning to Karina's office, Todd commented on this feeling he had sensed. "There's an energy about the place. A vibe. And I see a very relaxed atmosphere with none of the stress or tension I have experienced at previous companies!"

"Ah," the Sales Manager spoke, "that's because we are proactive in managing our sales results. We constantly achieve and attain our growth targets, and avoid missing budgets. We therefore stay well clear of the additional stress and pressure that can be placed on the entire team."

"You mean there is a way to do this?" asked the naïve Todd. He had been on the receiving end of few 'budget shortfall' moments during his short career in sales, and knew he wanted to avoid them at all costs.

"Definitely. Now that you have met the crew, let's start to explore our sales process and philosophy."

"Yes, please," answered an eager Todd. "I have heard various stories about your systems and sales approach. Why do you believe M&S is so successful?"

"Very simple," Karina began. "We have based our sales approach on a series of universal laws, which we all live by on a daily basis. They underpin how we operate here at M&S. And have become a part of our culture and our daily language. They represent how we perform when it comes to managing our sales result, and our time.

You see, Todd, selling is one of the oldest professions in the world. There may be different ways of saying it, yet there is nothing new in this profession. Being productive and successful in the sales industry is about applying a series of universal facts. Underpinning principles, if you will, which, when practiced, ensure you will succeed. Ignore them and you will suffer the consequences."

"Sounds similar to Aldous Huxley's quote. He said 'Facts do not cease to exist because they are ignored'."

"Is that right? Well, there you go. The same applies to these laws. The so-called Tall Poppies in the sales industry don't ignore these laws. They understand these principles and put them to work."

"What are they?" enquired the keen new starter.

"Not so fast, Todd. This may surprise you, initially, but I do not intend sharing them all with you."

"Oh," Todd said, a little deflated. "Can I ask why not?"

"Because we are not like most companies out there that have the 'Made Two Order' induction training program!"

"Made to order?" repeated Todd.

"No, Made TWO Order," corrected Karina, holding up two fingers. She continued. "Most companies have an induction program which involves showing the person around, a quick greet-and-meet, then the formal hand-over. With a list of clients, a map of the territory, the keys to the company car, they are shown the way to the car park."

"Tell me about it," said Todd with a wince. "I was on the receiving end of that one in my last place of employment. But that does not explain the TWO Orders bit?"

"Simple," continued Karina. "About 5 days later, the Managing Director walks in and asks the Sales Manager how the new rep is going. Has he got any orders yet? And the reply is usually "Yes, two orders:
1. Get out and,
2. Stay out until you make a sale!"

"Too true," laughed Todd, "Way too true!"

"Well, we don't play that game around here. It's not a great recipe for sales success. We do know there are "Seven Universal Laws to Sales Success"©, and they have underpinned this company's growth over many years."

"You make them sound like they are alive and part of the team," commented Todd.

"Well, in a way they are. They are our friends, and they support us to achieve amazing results. They are as real as the law of gravity, let's put it that way."

"Gravity?"

"Yes. We cannot see gravity and yet, it is real. There are many examples of how people like engineers harness the law of gravity to make the job easier. You have most likely done it yourself. Point in case; you stumble home at 2am, slightly worse for wear due to the effects of alcohol. You find yourself at the base of your bed, and you let gravity take over as you fall into the security of your comfortable, yet strangely spinning bed. The law of gravity is working for you, making the job easier."

"Ohhh," mumbled Todd. "I will confess to having been there a few times!"

"You wouldn't be alone, I'm sure," replied Karina with a smile. "Now, imagine you are in the same 'under the influence' state, but you are away on holidays with a group of friends, and you have been assigned the top bunk. Now gravity is working against you! Perhaps it is on the fourth attempt, with some skinned shins as evidence of your previous tries, that you finally haul yourself into the cot.

These laws are just as real as the law of gravity. You may not be able to see them, but they are there. If you do not embrace them and acknowledge them, they will be quietly working against you, having a huge negative effect on your sales performance. Abide by them, apply them to your thinking process, and you will reap the benefits.

When you hear about them, you too will sense that these laws can become your trusted friends. Friends that will serve you well. But as I said, I am not going to tell you about them now. I have learnt the hard way that it's best if you discover them for yourself. It's more effective.

I have set up a series of meetings for you today and tomorrow. You need to interview each of the people you will meet. Each understands the "Seven Universal Laws to Sales Success"©. They use, or have used them daily. You will get a better feel for them when they are relayed to you by various people who are not only passionate about applying them, but are getting great results."

"Fantastic! I can see the logic in that. Will I be spending some time with you as well?"

"Indeed. I will introduce you to the second and fourth key laws. I also want to see you briefly after every interview, when I will expect you to tell me what you have learned. I want to ensure you have a solid grasp on each law before you proceed to the next. Each principle is an independent natural law of sales effectiveness, and yet, each one is also interdependent. You will come to understand this as we explore the links.

Better move it! You're already three minutes late for your first meeting!" stressed Karina. "Just down the corridor. Third door on the right."

Special Bonus Material

If you would like more information on the strategies, tools and techniques available to help you improve your sales performance and grow your business register at:

www.ianstephensspeaks.com

CHAPTER THREE

Getting and Staying Ahead of the Game!

Todd gingerly popped his head through the open door of an office shared by two Key Account Managers.

"Hi there," said a short guy, straining to reach a book high on the office bookcase. "You must be Todd. Welcome to M&S. I'm Larry, and this is my colleague Rosemary," he said, pointing to a lady tapping away on her laptop computer.

"Nice to have you on the team, Todd," commented Rosemary, as she stopped what she was doing. "We have been expecting you. No doubt our Tall Poppy Sales Manager is sending you on the same journey we had to make when we joined M&S?"

"It appears that way. I understand the two of you will be introducing me to the very first of the 'Seven Universal Laws of Sales Success'©.

He had taken out his journal and was ready to take notes.

"Yes. We will," Larry indicated. "But, first I need to just make one phone call and plant another seed. Perhaps you can kick off, Rosemary?"

Todd moved over to Rosemary's workstation and took a seat beside her desk. "Planting seeds? That's the second time this morning I've heard that phrase," he said.

"You'll hear it a lot around here. It is a common phrase we use which represents the first key law of sales effectiveness. We all acknowledge the law of the harvest around here. It is one of the keys to success in the sales industry."

"You mean the old adage that you reap what you sow?" questioned Todd.

"Spot on. Being a success in selling, is no different to being a farmer tilling the soil. Farmers are painfully aware that there is a limited window of opportunity to get the seed into the ground. A delay of just a few weeks can have a huge impact on the quality and the quantity of the crop when it is finally harvested in the months to come. The crop takes time to grow and to fully develop. And it needs to be nurtured. It is no different in sales. We must consistently be planting the seeds, so that the harvest will be fruitful."

"And I guess there are dire consequences later, if they don't get the seeding done," added Todd.

"Absolutely," agreed Rosemary. "After the way most sales people operate, I'm beginning to realize why all high-rise office buildings have windows you can't open! There is a better option. We just take a leaf out of Robert Louis Stevenson's book. He said,

'Don't judge each day by the harvest you reap,

but by the seeds you plant.'

You see, this law applies to life in general, not just sales. The consequences of a lack of activity, in any area of life, always show up later. There might be a time period during which it is not obvious, but eventually, the evidence shows itself. For example, if you eat the wrong types of foods, and avoid exercise for 3 months, it will show up around the waist line. If you take six months off, and procrastinate about finding a job, the results will be quite negative in relation to your savings account. If you get out of the habit of always prospecting and mining for new business, from existing or new clients, then there will be a slump in your sales. And it will show up after the typical lag period for you and your business. Let me explain....

I was having a meal with my brother and his sales manager last week. Interesting conversation. I asked the sales manager how business was going, and he told me sales were down by 8%. He then said he had pulled his entire team together for a conference the previous weekend, and given them the proverbial kick up the rear. It came with the clear message that the shortfall must be 'made up'. In fact, to quote his exact words: 'Achieving the 30th of June budget is not negotiable! Let's keep in mind that it is now late April!'"

"Oh dear," muttered Todd.

"Yes, oh dear indeed, and for more than one reason. I then asked him the average time it takes from first talking to a potential customer until the order lands.

At this point he got a little defensive. The guy thought I was having a shot at him for "not understanding the basics". He said they have tracked that time period since they first started the business. He stated it was an average of 6 months."

Todd frowned as Rosemary's point dawned on him. "Ohhhh dear".

"Exactly! This sales manager does not understand the first under-pinning universal law of sales effectiveness. It is now the end of April with only eight weeks to go until the end of the financial year. This particular business has a six month average **LAG FAC**tor, and yet he wants the team to pick up an 8% shortfall in eight weeks!"

"And, it won't happen will it?"

"Of course not. That would be the equivalent of planting a crop which takes six months to germinate and fully grow, but attempting to harvest the crop after only two months. The crop will fail to yield any-thing of commercial value, and the farmer and his family will go hungry!"

"I guess they could land a couple of orders," commented Todd.

"They might get lucky and land a couple of orders," agreed Rose-mary, "and yet, for that to happen they will need to have a very full pipeline with some opportunities that are about to come home.

"Now, can I ask you Todd, when do you think the results of all the team's 'highly motivated' activity over the next eight weeks will final-ly produce an order?"

"Next financial year!" stated Todd, as the full impact of Rose-mary's point hit home.

"Yes, most of it in October, at the end of the **LAG FAC**tor period of 6 months."

"So," commented Todd, "you're suggesting it is imperative we know, understand and track the average **LAG FAC**tor in our business?"

"Yes. If we don't, how can we proactively manage the sales results, and land our targets in the right financial year?"

With that said, Rosemary bought Todd's attention to a poster on the wall of the office. It contained a picture of a small poppy seed and a fully bloomed poppy flower.

"See the picture over here? There is a time period between when you first plant a poppy seed, until when you get the beautiful result of a fully bloomed flower."

"There sure is," interjected Larry, having finished his phone call. "As Rosemary mentioned, from the time a poppy seed is planted, 'til the flower grows and blooms, there is a **LAG FAC**tor. The same applies to most businesses regarding sales. It is the first of the Seven Universal Laws. Have a look at what is printed below the images in the poster."

Todd stood and walked towards the poster, and read out loud:

"THERE IS A **LAG FACTOR** BETWEEN ACTIVITY AND RESULTS".

Todd wrote this in his journal.

"I can see how this would have positive stress management implications in terms of knowing you are going to hit the budget," said Todd.

"Indeed," agreed Larry. "Here at M&S, we are very conscious of doing enough seed planting in a timely manner, so the result will land in the right financial year. We will reap the harvest in a timely fashion. We therefore proactively manage our activities so we are ahead of the game, instead of behind. Todd, have you ever played or watched competitive tennis?"

"Yes, I am a keen player," he enthused.

"Well then, you will know the psychological difference when you are winning 6-3, 6-2 and are 5-1 up in the third set! It is a very different position than being in the opponent's shoes. He or she has to play catch-up tennis, dealing with constant pressure of being behind the game. Most sales people play catch-up, never getting ahead of the game!"

"Or ahead of the **LAG FAC**tor, so to speak," commented Todd.

"You've got it," concluded Larry. "Show me a salesperson who is constantly landing their targets in a timely fashion, and I'll show you a salesperson who is proactively managing the **LAG FAC**tor."

Larry stood up and put on his jacket. "We'd better run, Rosemary, if we are going to make that appointment with 10 minutes to spare!"

"Uh huh, more 'seed planting' hey?" said Todd.

"You're a fast learner" said Rosemary, as she and Larry disappeared out the door.

Todd reflected on the conversation. "**LAG FAC**, the poppy seed and poppy flower. Always manage the **LAG FAC**tor," he repeated to himself, and finalised his notes in preparation for his trip back to discuss the concept further with his new sales manager. An avid reader and writer, he summarized his findings and then made his way back to present them to Karina.

"So, what have you learned, my young eager new-start?" Karina asked, as Todd strode back into her office. Todd swung his journal around and let her read his summary…

The 1st Universal Law of Sales Success…

1. LAGFAC…(THE POPPY SEED TO THE FLOWER)

There is always a **LAG FAC**tor between activities and results.

- ⅄ Proactively manage the **LAG FAC**tor between the initial activity and when the result lands
- ⅄ Plan and complete sufficient activity in advance of the **LAG FAC**tor

- ✓ Reduces stress and pressure
- ✓ Ensures targeted results are achieved in the right financial year
- ✓ Places you ahead of the game

SALES EFFECTIVENESS APPLICATION:

"Achieving sales results through proactive and timely activity."

"Don't judge each day by the harvest you reap,

but by the seeds you plant." ...*Robert Louis Stevenson*

Finally comes the dawning...

It is the activity I did yesterday,

that will create the results I get tomorrow!

Now it finally dawns on me...

there is usually a lag factor between the key activities I do,

and when the results come home to roost.

With the dawning comes the knowledge that

I must always pro-actively track and

be conscious of the average lag factor,

in order to ensure results happen in the right financial year!

Let's Get Practical

Applying the Law of the Lag Factor

I will acknowledge the **LAG FAC**tor law by making a commitment to implement the following steps:

*1. I will implement a manual or automated system (via our computer systems) to track and monitor the **LAG FAC**tor between my activities and my results. This will allow me to be proactive and ensure I achieve my monthly/quarterly or annual results,*

*2. Today I will commence an 'Activities' campaign knowing that it will generate some results in ___ weeks/months. (Insert your **LAG FAC**tor),*

3. When it is time for me to take some holidays/annual leave, I will ensure I have done sufficient activities in advance of my vacation, so the results will continue to flow whilst I am not here.

Special Bonus Material

If you would like more information on the strategies, tools and techniques available to help you improve your sales performance and grow your business register at:

www.ianstephensspeaks.com

CHAPTER FOUR

The Unrecognised Truth Behind Sales Success!

"Excellent Todd," exclaimed Karina. "Be a good **LAG FACtor** manager and you are on the pathway to being a Tall Poppy in the sales industry. It is one of the most important things to focus on. I get a sense that you understand that now."

"Certainly do," responded Todd, "and yet, are you saying it is more important than the results we get? The companies I have worked with before have had a constant focus on results: daily, weekly, monthly."

"Ahhh, interesting. I should have expected that you, too, would have been conditioned to focus on results. It isn't surprising given that 80% of the senior managers in organisations have an accounting or financial background! Hence this obsession with results. They can slice and dice the numbers anyway they want them - by product, by area, by customer demographics - you name it. But, ultimately, they all need a paradigm shift!"

"What do you mean when you say 'a paradigm shift'?" enquired a confused Todd.

"A change in thinking or mind-set. We have all been conditioned by our parents, upbringing, society and experiences, and therefore tend to close off to different ways of thinking. We make choices as to what we believe, and to us, these beliefs are real. These beliefs, and our values system, which reside in the sub-conscious realm, guide our behaviour and the results we achieve. They determine our current way of looking at the world. Paradigms are the filters through which we see the world. I tell you what - let me give you a great example."

Karina reached into her bookshelf and produced a copy of a book.

"I have had this little beauty of a book for some time now; 'The Seven Habits of Highly Effective People' by Stephen Covey. He cites this example:

Two battleships assigned to the training squadron had been at sea on maneuvers in heavy weather for several days. I was serving on the lead battleship and was on watch on the bridge as night fell.

The visibility was poor with patchy fog, so the captain remained on the bridge keeping an eye on all activities.

Shortly after dark, the lookout on the wing of the bridge reported, "Light, bearing on the starboard bow."

"Is it steady or moving astern?" the captain called out.

THE SEVEN UNIVERSAL LAWS OF SALES SUCCESS · 29

Lookout replied, "Steady, captain", which meant we were on a dangerous collision course with that ship. The captain then called to the signalman, "Signal that ship: we are on a collision course, advise you change course 20 degrees."

Back came a signal, "Advisable for you to change course 20 degrees."

The captain said, "Send, I'm a captain, change course 20 degrees."

"I'm a seaman second class," came the reply. "You had better change course 20 degrees"

By that time, the captain was furious. He spat out, "Send, I'm a battleship. Change course 20 degrees."

Back came the flashing light, "I'm a lighthouse."

We changed course.

"That would quickly change your thinking, wouldn't it?" questioned Todd.

"Certainly would. In the same way of thinking, you need to quickly change your conditioned thinking from 'results management' to 'activity management'. The paradox here is that if you take care of the required activities, the results will take care of themselves."

Todd captured Karina's point in his journal.

"And I guess we have to get the key activities done in advance of the **LAG FAC**tor in order to land the results in the right financial year?" enquired Todd, as he remembered Rosemary's example of her brother's sales manager.

"Dead right, you do. I give you this promise. As the Sales Director for M&S, I'll be asking you to manage the activities you do, because we have no control over the results."

"No control over results!!" exclaimed Todd. "How do you mean?"

"Well, think about it. The results we get are dependent on three factors: firstly, the market place. In other words, customers and what they are doing. We can't control them or their decision-making process. We can influence it, but we can't control it 100%. Secondly, our competitors, and what they are doing. We can't control them or their marketing decisions. They might decide to drop prices in order to buy market share; we can't control that!"

"We could influence them if we are a market leader - a 'Tall Poppy' in the industry, couldn't we?" asked Todd.

"Yes, again, we could influence, but we can't control them 100%. I once saw a major company decide to diversify into a new market, and they wanted to grow quickly. Instead of spending millions buying an existing company, they instead went to market and totally undercut the competition by 30% in order to buy market share. Once they had a solid existing client base, they started gradually increasing their prices. This is a classic example of how we actually have no real control over the results. The only thing we can control is the third factor – ourselves, and the level of activity we do which will produce the results! The winners of the gold medals for sales productivity are those who understand and proactively manage the second principle well.

"My father, the founder of this company, used to refer to this as the **ACTIFIR** principle. It is an abbreviation of the second universal law of sales effectiveness."

She pointed to a small but important plaque sitting front and centre of her credenza. It read...

Always manage the **ACTI**vities **FIR**st

"His philosophy was that those who win the race, and take gold at the Olympics, are the athletes who put in the hard work before the event. They too, focus on the activities and the training necessary to achieve the result. The result on the day, is ultimately a result of the activity done beforehand.

He also used to tell me regularly, 'If you think it is going to be hard to make 10 calls this week, imagine how hard it will be to make 20 calls next week!'"

"And I guess, to continue the 'Seed Planting/Harvest' analogy," Todd added, "We need to be consistent in planting the seeds so the harvest takes care of itself!"

"Exactly. And if you don't have the discipline to consistently do the necessary activity, then the 'It'll show up later' law applies."

"The 'It'll show up later' law?" questioned Todd, probing for more information.

"Yes. If you don't do the activity now it will always show up in the result at exactly the end of the lag factor."

"So," Todd continued, "You're saying to always maintain some prospecting activity on a regular basis, and that it is easier to maintain?"

"Spot on. In fact, let me give you the same advice I give all new-starts when they join the sales team."

With that she walked over to the coffee table where a small jug of coffee was brewing. She laid out a coffee cup in a saucer and then continued…

"Todd, imagine this coffee cup represents the time you have to do some hunting and prospecting sales activity." She poured coffee into the cup until it was about half full.

"Most new sales reps get out there and do some initial sales activity, but then they get to about this point, and they think they have done enough." She indicated to the half full coffee cup.

"Here's my advice," Karina said, continuing as she slowly poured more coffee into the cup. "Keep your foot on the sales activity accelerator; keep pushing forward with your sales activity until I say you can back off a little."

The coffee cup was now over three quarters full.

"So even at this point, don't stop. Even if you think you have done enough. Even when the cup is literally over-flowing!" She stopped talking and let silence make her point.

Todd watched as the coffee reached the rim of the cup and began to overflow. It poured down the side of the cup and commenced filling the saucer.

Todd glanced nervously at Karina expecting her to stop. But she didn't. She smiled back at him but continued. She only stopped once the coffee in the saucer was lapping at the saucer rim itself, and began bulging as if ready to over-flow the saucer.

"About now," said Karina, "You can ease back a little on the sales activity accelerator. If you heed my advice, your new business sales cup will also 'over-runneth' and you will create a stream of clients who will feed your pipeline for years."

"Wow, I get it," exclaimed Todd having enjoyed the highly visual demonstration, "And, if I focus on doing the **ACTI**vities **FIR**st I will always stay ahead of the **LAG FAC**tor," Todd said out aloud, as he made his journal notes. "I can clearly see that these two principles work hand-in-hand!"

Karina smiled. "Great. Why don't you go ahead and explain?"

"Well," pondered Todd, "I guess you could liken it to a plane taking off. If the pilot has not got the speed of the plane and the revs of the engine up to a certain thrust, by the time he reaches a critical point on the runway, he abandons the take-off. He knows, mathematically, he won't get the plane off the ground before reaching the end of the run-way! He will run out of room. Also, once he has passed this critical point, he is committed to take off. He has no choice. With the speed he is going, he will not be able to stop the plane before running out of space. Either way, it's the same with sales activity. If we haven't done enough activity in advance of the **LAG FAC**tor, we will not land the results in a timely fashion. The end of the month, or the end of the financial year are like the end of the run-way. If we don't get the activity happening, our sales result won't take off."

"Excellent analogy! It seems you are in tune with our thinking so far. Before you move on to your next appointment, what notes have you taken about the second key principle?"

Todd flipped his journal around and showed Karina his notes…

The 2nd Universal Law of Sales Success...

2.   **ACTIFIR (THE GOLD MEDAL)**

Always manage **ACTI**vities **FIR**st!

ᐱ Change the paradigm - focus on activities and the results take care of themselves

ᐱ Plan, complete and maintain sufficient activities in advance of the **LAG FAC**tor

✓ Results always follow activities

✓ Whilst you can't control 'results', you can always control the activities you do

✓ Reduces stress and pressure

SALES EFFECTIVENESS APPLICATION:
"Predicting results through the completion of the key activities."

"If you think it's going to be hard to make 10 prospecting calls this week, imagine how hard it will be to make 20 calls next week!!" Anon

"Take a lesson from the dictionary: Activity comes before Result!" Ian Stephens

Finally comes the dawning...

Every result achieved has been preceded by

an activity of some description!

Now it finally dawns on me*... we have been conditioned to place our focus on the results, when in fact, we have little control over them. There is also a need to balance our attention on the key activities which will produce the results.*

With the dawning comes the knowledge *that I must also create an activity plan, knowing that once implemented, the fruits of my labour will be rewarded with the desired results!*

Let's Get Practical

Applying the Law of Activities First I will acknowledge the **ACTIFIR** law by making a commitment to implement the following steps:

1.   I will vigilantly plan and complete an agreed small amount of activity every week, which will ensure the pipeline is always bubbling with new business opportunities,

2.   I will acknowledge Results targets and review my progress towards them, but I will also set myself "Activity Targets" i.e. Number of New Business calls made per week, number of quotes/proposals submitted to potential clients, Number of Networking events attended.

Special Bonus Material

If you would like more information on the strategies, tools and techniques available to help you improve your sales performance and grow your business register at:

www.ianstephensspeaks.com

CHAPTER FIVE

Time to Get a Handle on Time!

Next, Todd met with a Key Account Manager, Mark, who was immaculately dressed in a pin striped suit. He was an action type of guy who was very conscious of the value of his time. He was keen to get down to business. After the preliminary introductions and small talk, he said, "Let's get you up to speed on the third key law because I don't have a lot of time today. I have three appointments this afternoon which, I hope, will see three orders finally land. I have been trying to win these three potential clients for two years now."

"That's a healthy **LAG FAC**tor," observed Todd.

"It sure is. As a Key Account Manager, I also have a new-new target; new business from new clients. As such, I have always tended to concentrate on the top end of town. The big fish take longer to land, but we persist and continue to do the necessary activities to build rapport and get it happening. As Karina keeps telling us…"

"Yes, I know," interrupted Todd, "do the activities and the results will take care of themselves!"

"Exactly! Of course, if you wish to be successful in sales, you also need to be a master of the third universal law of sales success," pointed out Mark.

"And I suppose this one too is represented by some character or icon with a weird name?" commented Todd.

"Absolutely. They may seem strange at first, and yet, it is suprising how they manage to lodge themselves in our sub-conscious mind, and pop up just when we need to be reminded of the laws. Can I just encourage you to stay open to the process, and then be amazed at how they start to serve you well?"

"Oh, yes. I have a feeling these laws are going to become my best friends! What is the icon for the next law?" enquired Todd, keen to learn more.

"An alarm clock, actually" answered Mark. "But as the story goes, it was nearly a Grandfather clock."

"Why the change?" asked Todd.

"Well, as legend would have us believe, when the law was first documented, and the artist commissioned to come up with a representation of the principle, Karina's father, the founder of the company, thought highly of the idea of a Grandfather clock; you know, suggesting this was an antique law as such. But then someone mentioned they had a Grandfather clock which didn't work well. Apparently all it did was wake up every hour, dribble, pass wind, and then go back to sleep! After that, old Jack went off the idea of a Grandfather clock, and decided on an alarm clock."

The two of them laughed together before getting back down to business.

"Todd, would you agree, we live in a world where time seems to be compressing? Generally, most of us wish there was more time in the day, and we are left wondering where this thing called time goes?"

"You are reading my mind!" laughed Todd.

"Good, you feel the same way. Well, let's understand more about time in the context of being in a sales role. There are basically five types of time," said Mark handing Todd a sheet containing a summary. Todd read through them carefully…

1. **Direct selling time**. *This is time with the decision-maker. Face to face, belly to belly.*

2. **Indirect selling time**. *Time with the influencers who may have some say in the decision.*

3. **Administration time**. *Doing the paperwork and the monthly reports.*

4. **Traveling and waiting time**. *This can be a killer. Time in the car getting to and from appointments, and time you lose waiting for the decision-maker to see you.*

5. **Personal time**. *Time for lunch, personal phone calls and the like."*

"Personal time, hmm?" commented Todd. "We had one person at my last company who thought because his hair grew on company time, it should therefore be cut on company time!"

Mark laughed along with Todd. "An excellent example of how we lose valuable time," he confirmed. "In fact, I often wonder just how much personal time impacts on our available time in the day. I know we have to balance life, and deal with personal phone calls and the like, but time does add up. I tell you what, why don't we understand how much time there actually is. Here's a form which will help us get a better grasp of just where all our time goes".

He produced a piece of paper and together they filled out the first part…

Time Analysis: Part One

No. of days in the year:			365
Less:	Weekends		104
		Leaves:	261
Less:	Holidays/Annual leave days		20
		Leaves:	241
Less:	Public Holidays		11
		Leaves:	230
Less:	Sick Leave		8
		Leaves:	222
Less:	Training/Conferences		10
		Leaves:	212
Less:	Miscellaneous (Trade Shows etc,)		8
		Net available days:	204

@ 10 hours per day = 2040 available hours per year.

"So, we only have about 200 days in the year to do the activity that produces the results!" exclaimed Todd.

"Yes, and at an average of 10 hours day, that's 2000 hours per year. Not a lot of time! And yet, it gets worse! Let's now examine the things which steal valuable time from us."

They looked at the second part of the form...

Part Two: Time Stealers Analysis

Admin & Paperwork: 2 hrs per day x 204 days = 408 hours

Traveling & Waiting: 2 hrs per day x 204 days = 408 hours

Meetings: ½ hrs per day x 204 days = 102 hours

Lunch breaks: ½ hrs per day x 204 days = 102 hours

Personal time: ¼ hrs per day x 204 days = ..51 hours

Total Time Stealers: 1071 hours

Total available hours per year: 2040

Less: Total Time Stealers: 1071

Net Available Hours per year: **969**

"Wow, we're down to just 969 hours," observed Todd.

"Yes, and that represents the time we have left for 'Direct selling time' and 'Indirect selling time', numbers one and two of the five types of time we discussed earlier. Everything else has been deducted and accounted for. When I showed this to a new colleague last year, she let out a four letter word starting with F!"

"What... FEAR?" added Todd with a sly smile.

"Nearly," laughed Mark. "So, the conclusion being the third key principle of effective sales productivity..."

He pointed to a poster on his wall which read...

SELling TIMe is LIMited!

"An alarm clock called **SELTIMLIM?**" queried Todd as he spotted the highlighted letters. "The actual time left over to sell is very limited, so place your focus on direct selling time with decision makers?"

"Exactly."

"And, I guess the alarm clock is an excellent picture, because if I am not focusing on the correct activities, alarm bells should start ringing?"

"Very good! Listen, I have to go to these appointments now. Good luck on your journey to discover the remaining principles. I look forward to working with you".

With that Mark was gone, and before long, Todd was presenting his journal notes to Karina...

The 3rd Universal Law of Sales Success...

3.   SELTIMLIM (THE ALARM CLOCK)

SELling **TIM**e is **LIM**ited

- ⋏ Focus on "direct selling" time with decision-makers
- ⋏ Be aware of time stealers
- ⋏ Avoid procrastination

- ✓ Selling time is only approx. 33% of your day given other duties and tasks
- ✓ Every hour that passes increases the impact of the **LAG FAC**tor

SALES EFFECTIVENESS APPLICATION:
"Increased productivity through effective time management."

Finally comes the dawning...

Time stands still for no-one, and it is constantly slipping by!

Now it finally dawns on me...*there is very little time to concentrate solely on selling activities given the extra duties of the job.*

With the dawning comes the knowledge *that I must learn to minimise time consuming activities which erode the time I must spend in front of decision makers!*

Let's Get Practical

Applying the **Seltimlim** Law.

I will acknowledge that **SEL**ling **TIM**e is **LIM**ited, and respect the SELTIMLIM law by making a commitment to implement the following steps:

1.   I will book time in my diary every day or week to do the key selling activities, which drive the sales results,

*2.   I will learn to say NO to procrastination, knowing every day that passes impacts on or extends my **LAG FAC**tor,*

3.   Today I will commence a four-week 'Time Awareness' exercise by keeping a log of where my time goes, and the tasks I do.

Special Bonus Material

If you would like more information on the strategies, tools and techniques available to help you improve your sales performance and grow your business register at:

www.ianstephensspeaks.com

CHAPTER SIX

Achieving the Right Balance!

"Excellent summary! What are the linkages between the three principles so far?" inquired Karina.

"Very simple. If I don't manage the limited amount of time well, I will find myself without enough runway! I won't have enough time to do the activities in a timely manner. The lag factor will now be working against me."

"Right! Excellent work. I sense from your enthusiasm for this learning process, that you are getting the profoundness of the laws. Let's you and I spend some more time together, and I will tell you about the fourth law. We need the flipchart, so let's move into the board room."

They made their way next door, and Todd turned to a fresh sheet in his notebook. When he was ready, Karina started to share more of the wisdom instilled in her by her father.

"Dad was a sales dog from way back. He was one of the best performing sales people in the history of M&S, because he understood and lived by all the laws. If you are interested in an additional principle which focuses on all the areas of the sales process, and increases your assertiveness, then take good notes."

"All this is certainly sparking my interest. What is the next law about?" enquired Todd.

"This one is a universal law, and a process model which governs our thinking process as to where we spend our time. It has pride of place in our monthly sales meetings and is the key model behind our success. We have grown to be a market leader in our industry, and can thank the principles for that. They soon become your friends. Used wisely and as a common system and language throughout an organisation, they propel you to sales success and achievement."

"So, please share with me the fourth law! I'm getting impatient here!"

"Okay. In the sales world, if you want to attain tall poppyship status and avoid stress, pressure and depression, it is essential to **MAIN**tain a **BAL**ance of focus on activity in various areas."

Karina walked to the flipchart in the boardroom, and turned a page over. It listed the three points emblazoned in the centre of the sheet...

1. Prospecting activity

2. Securing activity

3. Retaining activity

"Let me explain what normally happens to someone new like your-self, Todd. You're eager and keen to get out there and do some selling, so you get stuck into doing some 'Prospecting Activity'. You keep at it and guess what happens after the **LAG FAC**tor period?"

"Results occur. I get some orders!" said Todd enthusiastically.

"Exactly. You also start to get a pretty full pipeline of opportuni-ties, and turn your attention to doing 'Securing Activity'. This is the second or third visits where you are trying to secure the opportunity. This now starts to take up some of your time. When you start getting lots of sales, you suddenly have 'clients'. What do clients demand of you, Todd?"

"Service, I guess."

"You guess correctly, and service takes?"

"Time?" said Todd.

"Yes. You have ongoing service needs and problems, which take time to manage. You must therefore dedicate some of your time to 'Servicing and Retaining Activity'. Regretfully though, an unfortunate thing seems to happen in the psyche of most sales people. You focus on the 'Servicing and Retaining Activity' too much!'

"Why?" asked Todd.

"Because it is easier to do. Success in sales is easy if you obey the laws. It is also easy not to succeed in sales, because it is easy to abuse these laws. Let me explain what typically happens in the overall sales process.

You go and call on existing clients because you know them. It is more difficult to do 'Prospecting Activity'. That's too much like hard work, and it is normally outside people's comfort zones. Besides, existing clients know how you like your coffee, and you know when they are having scones for morning tea! It is far easier, psychologically, to go see existing clients than it is to find and land a new one. "

"I see," said Todd. "So the key is to **MAIN**tain **BAL**ance in the three areas?"

"It's more than that. It's about maintaining the required balance, the shape that will ensure the result is achieved. Let me show you on the flipchart.

Let's say you have to build a business from scratch. You have no clients at all. The shape of your wheel, in terms of where you will need to spend your time would be like this..."

Karina drew the following diagram on the flipchart:

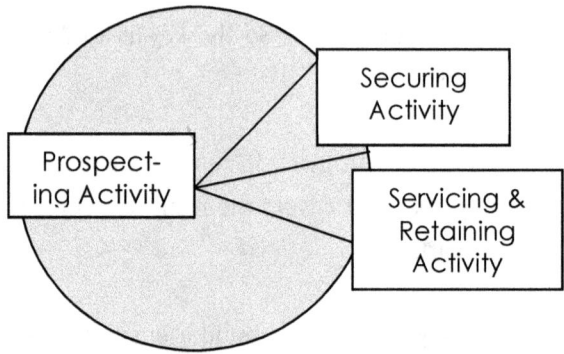

"That makes sense. I will need to spend all my time initially doing prospecting activity," agreed Todd, "because I have no customers to service."

"Dead right. Now, what would be the shape of the wheel in three months time, assuming you have a six month **LAG FAC**tor?" enquired Karina, keen for this young man to make the connections.

"I would hopefully have some business opportunities in the pipeline, so I would need to focus some attention, and time, on getting them over the line. I guess I would still dedicate a lot of time to prospecting activity?" suggested Todd.

"Correct. So, the shape of the wheel at this point would be this." as she drew the next shape on a new piece of flipchart paper.

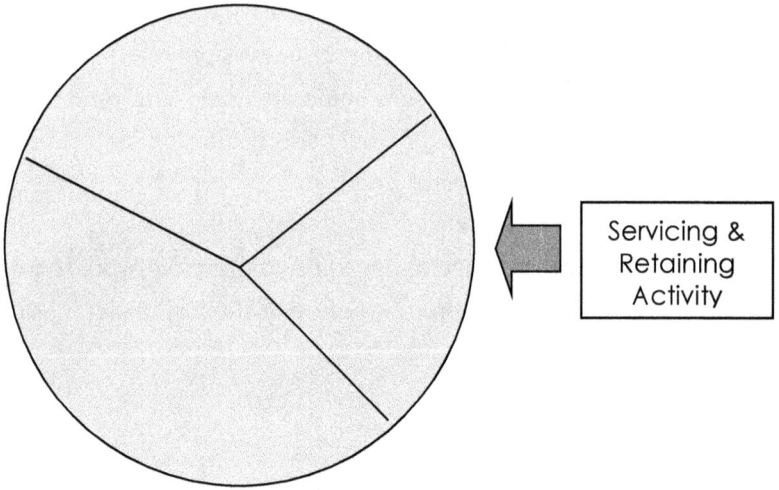

Servicing &
Retaining
Activity

"Note I have indicated a little time to 'Servicing and Retaining' activity, because you will have got lucky and landed some clients by now!"

'Yes," commented Todd, "Isn't it funny how good luck favors those who put in the hard yards?"

"Definitely, and it's no accident! That's the universal truth of the **ACTIFIR** principle which applies to any area of life: do the activities, and the results will follow. Luck plays a role, but it is predicated on hard work.

Okay, so now, Todd, what would the shape of the wheel be if you have been building and servicing the area for three years?" Karina asked, handing Todd the flipchart pen.

"Well," said Todd, as he took the pen from Karina, "I would suggest it should look something like this:

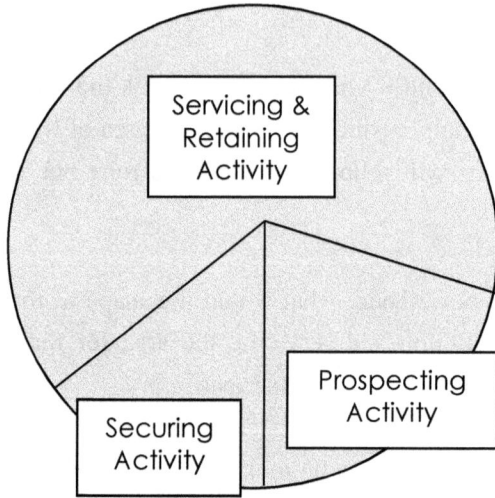

Servicing &
Retaining
Activity

Prospecting
Activity

Securing
Activity

"I will continue to 'Prospect' and 'Secure', and yet, the more substantial amount of my time would be dedicated to 'Servicing and Retaining' my client base."

"Excellent! I agree that's the shape it 'should' be, if you are still required to achieve growth. However, can I show you the shape that most sales people adopt after a while?"

"Sure," said Todd, handing back the pen.

"Here it is."

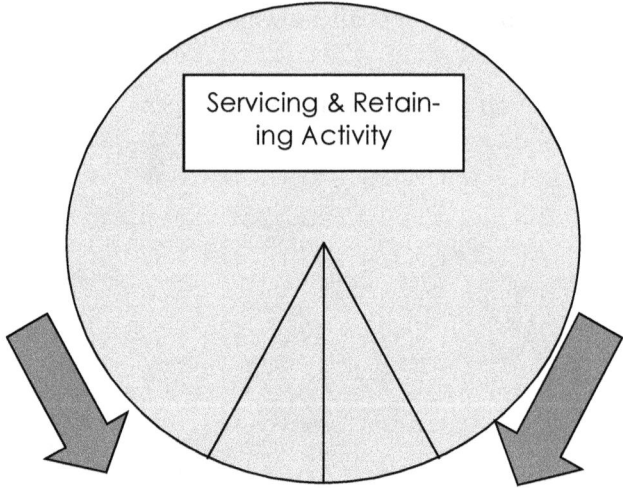

Servicing & Retaining Activity

"You see, most fall into the trap I mentioned earlier. They forget to **MAIN**tain the required **BAL**ance to achieve the desired results. The expansion of their customer base means more pressure on reducing the other two areas."

"I see," muttered Todd, as he made notes. In fact, he did see. "If I don't maintain balance, I will soon find no new business opportunities in the pipeline, and if I am also losing some customers to the competition, I will really be in trouble!"

"Trouble, with a capital T!" confirmed Karina. "So, update me. What did you learn from **MAINBAL**?"

Todd flipped to the latest page in the journal...

The 4th Universal Law of Sales Success...

4.   **MAINBAL**   (THE WHEEL)

MAINtain **BAL**ance in all selling areas!

- ⊼ Marketing activity (prospecting)
- ⊼ Working activity (securing)
- ⊼ Servicing and retaining activity

- ✓ Ensures we never lose focus on one area of the wheel
- ✓ Creates a foundation for ongoing sales success
- ✓ Develops assertiveness in saying "NO" to less important tasks

SALES EFFECTIVENESS APPLICATION:
"Consistent achievement through consistent balance of activities."

Finally comes the dawning...

To be successful in the sales industry, I must have the balance of a tight rope walker!

Now it finally dawns on me... *I must balance my attention and focus on doing the required amount of prospecting, securing and retaining activity, if I am going to stay ahead of the game.*

With the dawning comes the knowledge *that I must always reflect on the week or month gone by, and plan the type and amount of activity moving forward, which will guarantee success!*

Let's Get Practical

Applying the **MAINBAL** Law

I will acknowledge the **MAINBAL** law by making a commitment to implement the following steps:

*1.   I will review the shape of my **MAINBAL** wheel every week. This will involve drawing two circles and comparing the shape of the wheel from last week, with the shape it needs to be to ensure my sales targets are reached,*

*2.   Today I will slightly increase the time I spend in the Prospecting piece of the **MAINBAL** pie, knowing this will create a new wave of momentum and sales,*

*3.   I will be pro-active in arranging a monthly meeting with my one-up to discuss the **MAINBAL** shape required, and agree a forward sales activity plan.*

Special Bonus Material

If you would like more information on the strategies, tools and techniques available to help you improve your sales performance and grow your business register at:

www.ianstephensspeaks.com

CHAPTER SEVEN

The Science of Reverse Planning

"Terrific," said Karina. "Next, I've got a surprise arranged for you. You're spending an hour with my father."

"You're joking," exclaimed Todd, "The founder of M&S?"

"Yes, but retired now. And relax. He's a human being just like you and me. And underneath his tough exterior, he is a teddy bear at heart. He keeps himself busy travelling the world with Mum."

"Spending the inheritance, eh?" enquired Todd.

"Absolutely. And good luck to them. They have earned it. Although I do occasionally remind them to be nice to me; I will ultimately control the quality of nursing care they receive!"

"Where am I catching up with him?"

"Here. He's meeting a few of his old friends and has agreed to spend some time with you. He is absolutely passionate about the 5th universal law of sales productivity and success. If you want to hear about a simple diagnostic tool which allows you to know how much activity is required to produce a result, then listen to Jack's message."

"Can't wait. Where is he?" enquired Todd.

"In the staff coffee lounge. And remember, his bark is worse than his bite. He just tells it how it is. No shades of grey with my father, so don't take any offense if he is a bit direct on a few points. And heed his advice. In his younger days he was tough on people who did not implement the 5th law".

When Todd entered the lounge, he instantly knew whom he was meeting. Jack had a presence about him, and a group of people were hovering around him, hanging on his every word.

"What a pleasure to meet you, sir!" said Todd, after the formal introductions were completed.

"Drop the formalities, young fella. Jack's the name, although I have been called a few other things in my time".

Todd laughed and immediately felt at ease. They sat down in a comfy lounge opposite one another.

"I hear you want to be a success in the sales world" Jack stated.

"Yes. I set out to get a job here because I heard M&S has a sales methodology that supports success, instead of making it an uphill battle! I mentioned to Karina that there is an energy about the place. None of the stress I have seen in prior companies I have worked for."

"That's because the pressure is off," said Jack. "I was just chatting to a few of the team. They have done the required level of activity in the last six months, and now the results are flowing in. They have won enough contracts to secure the results for the next 12 months, and there's heaps more in the pipeline."

"No doubt this is because they have applied and lived the principles I have been learning. Can you share the 5th principle with me? I know it must be a hum-dinger. Karina says you are passionate about it!"

"It is a very simple yet profound process of knowing exactly how much activity needs to be done in order to secure the sales result. But Todd, before we begin, what sort of car do you prefer? Manual or automatic?"

"A manual. Feels like I am more engaged in the process of driving. And in any event, I agree with a quote I once read by a P.K Shaw; The problem with automatic cars is that they're still driven by manual brains!"

Jack laughed. "I like your humour, Todd. Tell me, which gear do you think is the most powerful in a standard car?"

"Probably third gear I guess. Most torque?"

"Really?" with a slightly surprise toned and a quizzical look.

"Well, actually…" stammered Todd, "I guess I don't really know."

"Then don't make it up, young fella. Let me give you a quick bit of advice before we get down to discussing the next law. There was a magician performing on an around-the-world cruise ship, but each time he arrived at the climax of his trick, a passenger's parrot would give the secret away. As the magician started yet another illusion there was a thunderous explosion. When the smoke had cleared the magician and the parrot were alone together on a make-shift raft floating in the ocean. After three days of silence the parrot spoke up. "OK," he said, "I give up, what the hell did you do with the blasted ship?"

Todd let out a nervous laugh knowing Jack still had a point to make.

"No shame in not knowing the answers, Todd. But for heavens sake, as a new person on board at M&S, don't be like the parrot and sit in silence thinking you know what other people might be talking about. Always best to ask good questions instead of making it up!"

"Okay. Fair call."

"Good. Now back to the car gear stick. Ask Henry Ford, and he will tell you the most powerful gear in the second T model Ford ever built was the reverse gear."

"Reverse!"

"Yes, apparently in the excitement of designing the T Model Ford, he forgot to include a reverse gear. Henry went to work and made sure he fixed that quick smart. In fact, the reverse gear in the second model was considered more powerful than any of the other gears in the car. Back in those days, when the roads were dirt tracks, and the weather was wet, it was not uncommon for people to tackle muddy hills in reverse."

"Really?" exclaimed Todd in a slightly mocking tone which imitated Jack's earlier comment.

Jack paused a moment, glanced at Todd, then smiled. Not a bad kid he thought to himself. Very quick witted. He continued.

"Like the early Model T Ford owners, the most successful sales professional tackles their sales targets by getting in reverse! I have trained all the Key Account Managers in M&S, to write down the result they want, and then...

Create a
'REVerse
PLAn'

'A **REV**erse **PLAn**" repeated Todd as he captured his notes.

"Yes, this allows you to clearly see how much activity needs to happen to achieve the result. Just work it in reverse. Let me explain.

Let's say I want to achieve $100,000 sales in the next 12 months. I look at the average size of the order. Let's say it's $10,000. How many orders do I need?"

"Ten," said Todd.

"Okay, so now I reverse the plan even further. If I need ten orders, I then do an analysis of my conversion rate (which I track) of quotes to orders. I know that's a 2:1 conversion."

"So, in other words, you win one of every two you quote or tender for?"

"Yes. So, that means I need to get 20 quotes out there in order to win ten. If I back up the plan even further, what is the main activity I will need to do to get in a position where I can provide a quote?"

"Umm, prospecting visits or appointments, I guess!"

"Correct! So, I now look at my ratio of 'visits to quotes'. I know that's three to one. On average, I get one opportunity to quote, every three appointments. So..."

"I get it," interrupted Todd. "At a 3:1 ratio, you need 60 appointments to achieve 20 quotes. At a 2:1 ratio of 'quotes to orders', that will give you the ten orders, which at $10,000 each supplies the $100,000 sales result!"

"Spot on! Of course, your **REVerse PLAn** may need to go further. Not everyone will agree to a visit, so if my ratio of 'phone calls to appointments in the diary' is 5 to 1, I need to make 300 phone calls. Of course, the decision-maker you want to talk to may be out. Sometimes, I have to persist and call 5 times to get to reach the decision-maker, so that equates to about 1500 dials on the phone!!!"

"And that's way too much," Todd muttered, working through the figures.

"In one hit, yes. It's too many phone calls when you have other things to do. But in small continuous doses, very manageable. See, this is where the other principles come into play. **REVPLA** allows you to determine the amount of activity required, so you can plan it, and do it in advance of the **LAG FAC**tor."

"So, this is why the team appears so relaxed. The result they want is already in the bag!"

"That's right," confirmed Jack. "If you wish to continuously achieve budgets, and avoid the highs and lows that typically accompany this industry, become a person who works in reverse. Otherwise, the only other option I know of is the S.W.A.G. method!"

"The SWAG method?" asked Todd, unable to resist.

"Yes. When it comes to achieving the sales target, it's either the **REVerse PLAn** process, or you take a finger, place it in your mouth, hold it up to the wind, and take a **S**imple **W**ild **A**rse **G**uess as to what you will achieve!"

Todd roared with laughter.

"Jack, thanks so much for your input. I will implement the knowledge, and put it to work for me, and the company."

"I know you will, young fella," finished Jack, glancing at his watch. "You go do that. As for me, I'm off home. It might only be 2pm here, but I'm positive it's got to be a five o'clock happy hour somewhere in the world! I need a scotch!"

With that, Jack disappeared, and before long Todd was placing his summary in front of Karina...

The 5th Universal Law of Sales Success...

5.   REVPLA   (THE GEARSTICK IN 'R')

Always create a **REV**erse **PLA**n.

- ⅄ Determine target result...then reverse plan the required level of activity
- ⅄ Understand and track your key conversion ratios

- ✓ Determines the type and amount of activity required to produce the desired result
- ✓ Allows proactive planning of resources
- ✓ Reduces stress and pressure

SALES EFFECTIVENESS APPLICATION:
"Achievement of desired results through implementing necessary activities."

"Show me a salesperson who can consistently achieve targets, and I'll show you a salesperson who understands and completes the required activities to produce the result!".........
Ian Stephens

Finally comes the dawning…

Sales is simply a numbers game, and I must know my key conversion ratios!

Now it finally dawns on me*… to operate without a Reverse Plan, and without an understanding of my ratios, is to operate completely in the dark.*

With the dawning comes the knowledge *that I must always create a solid Reverse Plan, and then implement the activity, which will create the results!*

Let's Get Practical

Applying the **REVPLA** Law

I will acknowledge the **REVPLA** law by making a commitment to implement the following steps:

> 1.   *I will set up a system (manual or electronic), which starts to capture and track my key conversion ratio's. I understand it will take three times the **LAG FAC**tor before I have complete confidence in the ratio's, but the confidence will come,*

> 2.   *I will sit down in the next 24 hours and create my 1st draft **REV**erse **PLA**n. This will at least give me an understanding of the activity levels required to generate the sales result.*

Special Bonus Material

If you would like more information on the strategies, tools and techniques available to help you improve your sales performance and grow your business register at:

www.ianstephensspeaks.com

CHAPTER EIGHT

Small Changes Create Big Results!

"Great Todd. I will want to hear all about your **REVerse PLAn** by the end of next week. Now it's time for you to meet with an old mentor of mine," said Karina.

"He no longer actively works within M&S, and yet, he and my father are very close friends and were business partners. Jay is a retired director of the company and has always instilled in us the sixth universal law of sales effectiveness. I have arranged for you to meet with him at his home. A driver is waiting for you outside."

After a brief journey Todd found himself sitting in a beautiful lounge room in a glamorous home. Waiting for Jay to join him, he noticed a archery bow with a quiver of arrows displayed in a glass case. He was inspecting it more closely when Jay made his way into the room, introduced himself, and they got underway.

"I see you have already found SMACHABI, the Bow and Arrow. She represents the law I have been asked to share with you" Jay commented.

"Excellent. I have spent the day so far learning about the other five. I take it this one too will be essential to learn and apply."

"Only if you are looking to continuously improve both yourself and the results you achieve," replied Jay.

"I certainly am," enthused Todd. "So the key lies with this bow and arrow?"

"Indeed. Her name is **SMACHABI**, and she is an acronym for:

SMAll CHAnges....
create BIg results!

I have never subscribed to a philosophy of making major changes. I believe success comes from a process of continuous and never-ending improvement. If you track for the minor changes that will create major results, I believe you are on a pathway to success."

"Minor changes, major results," repeated Todd.

"Yes. Are you aware of the percentage amount of time that a space shuttle is actually on track to arrive at the destination?"

"No. But I would assume it must have been most of the time?" answered Todd.

"No. Most people are shocked to learn it is less than 3% of the time. NASA Mission Control and the astronauts are constantly making minor adjustments to the trajectory, firing rockets and thrusters continuously in order to ensure the final destination is achieved. A small change could mean the difference between hitting the target and missing it altogether. It's exactly the same with any aero plane. The auto pilot is constantly analyzing the effects of winds and weather conditions, and making small adjustments to the direction of the aircraft. If it didn't, these outside influences would nudge the craft slightly off course. Compound these small nudges over the duration of the flight, and who knows where you might end up."

"Yes, and I have another example," said an excited Todd. "I have a cousin in the marine industry. He is studying to gain his next level of qualifications so he can skipper an ocean liner. He was telling me about the 'Trim Tab'. This is like a small rudder contained within the major rudder. When they want to turn the ship, they make a minor adjustment to the trim tab, which displaces some water, and makes it quicker and easier to turn the major rudder. The result is a massive improvement in the response time of the ship and the size of its turning circle!"

"Same principle," confirmed Jay. "Make minor adjustments and results soar! I have always suggested to the M&S sales team that massive changes are tough to make, whereas small or minor adjustments are very manageable."

"I think I know where you are coming from, Jay" commented Todd. "It is not hard to increase from 5 calls a day to 6, yet very hard psychologically to increase to 20 calls a day!"

"Yes. And how would the results change, if you looked at your **REVerse PLAn**, and were able to just make a minor improvement in your conversion ratio from 3:1, to 2:1?"

"The amount of activity required to achieve the result would reduce dramatically!"

"Sure would. You see, when we harness the compound effect over a long time-frame, minor adjustments equal big results! Show me a sales person who is continuously improving both personally and professionally, and I will show you a sales person who understands and applies the **SMACHABI** Principle."

"But why a bow and arrow to represent this law?" asked Todd.

"Simple" explained Jay. He took Todd over to a TV and press play on a pre-prepared recording of a group of archers.

"Observe the process the archers are going through the motions of during their practice session."

One particular archer was not doing as well as the others. Most arrows were hitting the third ring out from the bulls-eye. Todd observed an official looking guy, perhaps the coach, go over to assist the struggling archer. Todd couldn't hear the conversation, but he got the gist of what the coach was doing. He was demonstrating to the archer how to make a slight adjustment in the direction of the arrow, and a small shift in the way he held the bow. Following his coach's instructions to the letter, the archer proceeded to fire his next six arrows, all of which found their mark somewhere in the bulls-eye.

The link to the seventh law was dawning on Todd. He turned back to Jay. "It is a classic metaphor for your small changes thinking. At the distance they must fire, and the elite level at which Olympic archers compete, an absolutely minor change in direction has a massive impact on the results. Small change... Big results!"

Jay beamed. "You've got it. Notice also the subtle coaching with the position of the bow. There is rarely one large 'silver bullet', Todd. The answer generally lies in finding the one small thing you can do differently, which when harnessed with the power of time and the law of consistency, add up to a massive result."

"So, from a sales and customer service perspective," mentioned Todd, "We should look for the twenty 1% improvements in our practices or skills, as distinct to the one thing we can do 20% better?"

"Hey, do both if you can," encouraged Jay, "And yet in my experience, in this day and age, most major changes have been located and made. The answer now usually lies in identifying the minor adjustments. You see, when we harness the compound effect over a long time-frame, minor adjustments equal big results! Show me a person, team or organisation who is continuously improving, and I will show you an individual, or a team, who understand this seventh law – Small changes, create big results. I don't know who is behind this quote, but it applies to this thinking:

"Often the biggest changes in life are a result of something small. A subtle catalyst that sets into motion a chain of events, which alters the course of action, and therefore, the results."

During his trip back to the office, Todd completed his summary notes for Karina. Within fifteen minutes, he was back at the office displaying his notes for Karina to review.

The 6th Universal Law of Sales Success...

6. SMACHABI (THE BOW AND ARROW)

SMAll **CHA**nges....**BI**g results!

⋏ Find small changes which will create big results over time
⋏ Track for continuous improvement

✓ Small changes are manageable
✓ Most massive changes have been made
✓ Harness the effect of compounding over time

SALES EFFECTIVENESS APPLICATION:
"Improved results through focusing on minor adjustments."

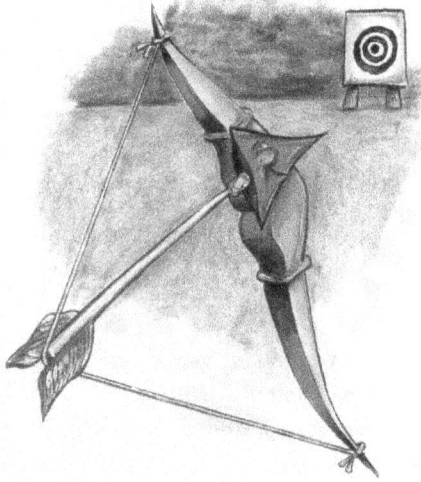

"One small step for man. One giant leap for mankind."

Neil Armstrong

Finally comes the dawning…

That I should harness the nature and effect of compounding over time!

Now it finally dawns on me*…the answer lies not in making massive changes, but in listening to wisdom's quiet whisperings and finding the few small changes which will create the biggest results.*

With the dawning comes the knowledge *that I must always track for the one or two small adjustments, which when coupled with the magnificence of time, will create staggering result!*

Let's Get Practical

Applying the **SMACHABI** Law

I will acknowledge the **SMACHABI** law by making a commitment to implement the following steps:

1.   I will ponder, identify and list the three or four small things I can do differently or improve in order to produce better results,

*2.   I will tell others about the **SMALL CHANGES** I am going to make, knowing that my commitment and resolve increases once others are made aware of my intentions,*

3.   I will adopt a continuous improvement mentality, and ask for feedback regularly, from peers and leaders, on the few things I could change that would have a dramatic impact on my personal and professional life.

Special Bonus Material

If you would like more information on the strategies, tools and techniques available to help you improve your sales performance and grow your business register at:

www.ianstephensspeaks.com

CHAPTER NINE

Success breeds success!

"Well, Todd, you are nearing the end of your 'universal sales laws' discovery journey," said Karina.

"Yes, but only about to commence the journey of applying them," replied Todd.

"Before you start that journey, I have one more person for you to meet and learn from. She is an interstate Key Account Manager for M&S, and, she's in town today attending a supplier's product launch later. She is waiting in Rosemary's office for you."

With that, Todd was on the move again. Rebecca was with Larry and Rosemary when he walked in. She quickly wrapped up the discussion and made her way over.

"Hi there, Todd! Rebecca's the name. Nice to have you with us at M&S."

"Thanks," said Todd. "And thanks for making time to see me. I understand you have been charged with the challenge of getting me up to speed on the final key law which I must learn before putting my knowledge into practice."

"Easy. Come with me," she said, as she walked out of the office, left the building and did not stop until she was sitting on the top of a nearby hill in the park opposite the office.

"Boy, you're energetic," exclaimed a puffed and confused Todd, who had struggled to keep up with this ball of energy.

"That's what this principle is all about. Creating energy. I like to **CREA**te some **MOM**entum, and keep it going."

"Ah ha, Create Momentum," scribbled Todd. "And I bet the name of the law is **CREAMOM**, or maybe Creamomtum, or perhaps Cretum?"

"Dead right the first time. **CREAMOM**. You've certainly got a handle of the naming process! Todd, have you ever had one of those days where everything goes your way? When everything you touch turns to gold, and you really create some momentum with the tasks you are doing?"

"Sure," confirmed Todd. "It's like you're in the zone. Everything goes your way. I've had those days where everything goes the other way, too. You know, where everything you touch turns to…"

"Indeed. We all have those. That's when it's time to change our 'state', and try and create some positive momentum."

Rising, Rebecca walked over to a nearby boulder laying on the crest of the hill.

"We use a boulder to represent this universal law. And I think you'll understand why in a moment." With that Rebecca wrestled to get the boulder upright on it's side. She had to work hard at getting it moving, and gave a groan as she really put her back into it. The boulder seemed to be winning the battle, but then all of a sudden, it began to move. As the slope of the hill increased, the boulder started to gain some momentum for itself.

"Come on!" yelled Rebecca back over her shoulder towards Todd. She shot off down the hill following the boulder which was now racing away down the slope.

Todd sprang into action and followed in hot pursuit. He witnessed the boulder increase its speed and power until it finally crashed into the wire mesh fence at the base of the hill, and came to a complete stop.

"I get it," gasped Todd, as he finally caught up with the Rebecca. "Create some momentum and it actually becomes easier!"

"Yes. It took some hard work and effort to get it moving, but once it gained some momentum, it took on a life of its own. The same applies in sales Todd. Create some momentum. Get active, and then keep the roll going. Success breeds success. I remember the very first time I landed a decent sized order, and phoned Karina to tell her about it. Her response was to suggest I get on the phone and make some cold calls!"

"Why?"

"Because having a win puts you in a great state of mind. Potential customers pick up on that. Whenever I do this, my conversion ratios improve also. I usually get two appointments per three calls instead of one. I'm on a roll and I know I can maintain that momentum.

The key message is to make sure you create and then maintain some momentum in all the **MAINBAL** areas."

"You mean prospecting, securing and servicing activity?"

"Very good, Todd. Yes. Constant small amounts of activity are easy to maintain. I sometimes see even the most seasoned sales professionals who get caught up in their results success, and forget to maintain some balance on the prospecting activity and securing tasks. They lose momentum in one or two of the **MAINBAL** areas. It really is about maintaining a level of momentum in all three areas."

"I can relate to that. Thank you, Rebecca. This has been really useful. I will **CREA**te some **MOM**entum and maintain it."

Todd wandered back up the hill and sat quietly under the shade of a gum tree whilst he updated his journal. About 15 minutes later, he returned to Karina's office and showed her his summary of the **'CREAMOM'** law…

The 7th Universal Law of Sales Success...

7.   CREAMOM   (THE ROLLING BOULDER)

CREate and maintain **MOM**entum.

- ⅄ "Success breeds success"
- ⅄ An increase in activity automatically multiplies the effect of each activity by the sheer nature of the momentum created
- ⅄ Future results are dependent on past activity and momentum
- ⅄ People sense the energy of a winner

- ✓ Constantly implement activity in all three areas (prospecting, securing, retaining)
- ✓ Capitalise on mental highs by immediately doing some prospecting activity
- ✓ "Ride the wave" of your current successes

SALES EFFECTIVENESS APPLICATION:
"Minimising the inertia typically associated with the peaks and troughs of the normal sales cycle."

"Show me a salesperson who never stresses about landing their budget, has an overflowing pipeline, and I'll show you a person who creates and maintains constant momentum."

Ian Stephens

Finally comes the dawning…

I am the master of my own destiny, and have the choice available to me at any time, to get active, and create some momentum!

Now it finally dawns on me… *momentum does not just happen. It is the result of an initial burst of motion, but has a trail of positive results.*

With the dawning comes the knowledge *that I am an energy force, and must harness the fact that 'success breeds success', and always be mindful of creating and maintaining some momentum!*

Let's Get Practical

Applying the **CREAMOM** Law

I will acknowledge the **CREAMOM** law by making a commitment to implement the following steps:

1.   I will immediately 'Get Active' and increase my activity levels for ___ weeks, knowing that this activity will be the catalyst of a new wave of future results,

2.   I will sit down and plan my Sales Activity for the next ___ weeks, then simply do it,

3.   Initiate a marketing campaign of some sort to my existing client base, in order to produce some referrals and/or additional business, which will create a new injection of sales opportunities into my pipeline.

Special Bonus Material

If you would like more information on the strategies, tools and techniques available to help you improve your sales performance and grow your business register at:

www.ianstephensspeaks.com

"Congratulations, Todd," said Karina. "You have been very studious in your endeavors with The Seven Universal Laws of Sales Success ©. You are now armed with the knowledge to be a great success, and a long term Tall Poppy in the sales profession.

Before you commence your product training, explain to me how the **CREAMOM** principle links to the others?"

"I have been thinking about that. I honestly believe that if I don't apply this principle then nothing will get done. I need to do some **ACTIFIR** in order to create the momentum necessary, which will lead to results. I then need to maintain some momentum in all areas of the **MAINBAL** model. This principle is like the glue, which binds all the others together. Without some momentum, nothing happens!"

"Right. So maybe it's time to put some of your new-found knowledge to work, because knowledge un-applied equals baggage!"

"Knowledge un-applied equals baggage?" queried Todd still taking notes.

"Yes. Let me read you a short passage out of this book", said Karina as she pulled a copy of 'The 7 Step Pathway to Mastery' by Ian Stephens and Roger Anthony, from her book shelf. She quickly turned to page 119 and started reading…

'There's a true story of a gentlemen who perished in the wilderness in a forest near Denver in the USA. He literally froze to death after becoming lost in rugged snow terrain. When the snow had melted and his body discovered, they examined the contents of his backpack. Amongst his possessions was a box of matches.

How sad that this man lost his life when the outcome could have been radically different. He only had to put his knowledge to work. Surely he knew that in order to protect himself from the cold, he needed to:

- Find himself a small cave or sheltered overhang out of the wind
- Collect some wood
- Build himself a fire
- Strike a match and light the fire

Yes, perhaps he became distraught and confused. Perhaps he simply forgot he had matches with him. Many of us go through life with the knowledge in our backpack! And yet, we don't strike the match of knowledge, against the flint of action. We fail to apply the knowledge we have within us."

"Todd, I'm impressed by your attitude to learning these laws. But it is time to now apply the knowledge, and go to work," said a pleased Karina. "Let's now commence some product training which will give you the confidence to go out into the market place and create results."

Epilogue...

And so it came to pass that Todd did apply the seven laws. They became his friends and support partners. And because of the learning methodology, and because the entire team understood the same tools, concepts and language, the laws popped into his mind when he needed them most. The laws and their names were a common language around M&S, and a regular feature at their sales meetings.

For the first three months of his sales career at M&S, Todd did little more than continual prospecting and securing activity. He heeded Karina's advice and kept the foot down on the 'Activity accelerator' until his cup and saucer was overflowing. At the end of the first quarter he spent some time analysing his ratios. He worked out his average conversion rate and prepared his **REVPLA**. By the end of the second quarter, Todd's pipeline was in good shape. He adjusted his level of new business prospecting activity accordingly and spent more time securing the opportunities in his pipeline. And yet, he did not make the fatal mistake of stopping the hunting activity altogether. He never let a week go by without scheduling some time in his diary to do some 'Seed Planting'. He had already seen two new sales employees underestimate the power of the **ACTIFIR** and **LAGFAC** laws, and they were currently under instruction from Karina to improve their activity levels. They were playing catch-up football, and did not like it!

Together Todd and his M&S team members, continued to grow M&S. As a company, they maintained their position as a market leader in their field. It was Todd who diligently applied himself to landing a major international account. He still has vivid memories of celebrating late into the night with his colleagues.

He produced and supplied his entire team with a colourful recall chart, which included all seven principles he had learned. A copy is included at the end of this book.

In years to come, Karina became the Chairman of the M&S board, and Todd was promoted to the role of Sales Director. In this role, he used "The Seven Universal Laws of Sales Success"© to manage, measure, monitor and coach his growing sales team.

Todd then went on a new quest to understand the key principles of being an effective sales-leader and coach.

After three years in the National Sales Managers role, word of his success, and M&S's sales methodology had spread. Todd received an invitation to speak at National Sales Managers forum. He was asked to deliver a keynote talk providing practical tips on how Sales Managers could guarantee the revenue result.

The paper he submitted and delivered at the seminar follows on the next four pages.

Landing the revenue result…and getting a good night's sleep!

What does a CEO, Managing Director, National Sales Manager or Regional Sales Manager all have in common? Answer: they all lose sleep over whether the promised revenue figures will occur. This article details the 4 key strategies organisations should be implementing in order to dramatically increase the chances that the forecast becomes a reality, and that you get a good night's sleep!

A recent survey of our senior executives revealed speaking in public is not the greatest fear of senior leaders. Whether or not the sales forecast would occur; this caused them to lose valuable zzz's. They, and the financial controllers, have confidence in such things as 'cost of sales', and they have done everything possible to remove unnecessary costs from the business. But the 'excel' spreadsheet, which has rolled up and down the organisational chart to determine the EBIT target, ain't worth the laptop it's stored on, unless the revenue actually occurs.

So how do you increase the chances that the targets will be achieved, and reduce that niggling doubt? How do you ensure the sales-force lands the sales result in a timely fashion, and avoid finishing 10% down? Finish 20% down, and there goes the EBIT line!

In my experience, the answer lies in the following 4 key points. For the CEO's and MD's who want the global summary, here it is:

1.   Shift your thinking…results are not the most important thing.
2.   Well Defined Marketing Direction with evidence that it is being executed by the sales-force.

3.   A well developed 'Pipeline' measurement and reporting process.

4.   Complete a Reverse Planning process to determine the level of activity required to produce the result.

For the National Sales Director and Regional Sales Managers who need to implement them, here is the detail:

1.   Shift your thinking…results are not the most important thing.

A majority of senior executives have an accounting background, and accordingly, have a tendency to focus on the results. And we can carve the numbers up any way we want them: by month, quarter, year, by product, area, region, state, etc, etc. My hobby is to politely get in their faces and point out the logical truth. Snap the paradigms if you like. Results only occur when it is preceded by an activity. For a result to happen, something has had to have happened! Be it a prospecting call, a meeting, a proposal/tender/submission. An activity of some description occurred that created the result. I remember a sales rep in the insurance industry during my days as an inexperienced Regional Sales Manager. I pulled out the monthly result sheet. He rolled his eyes back in his head and pointed out his sales philosophy, "Ian, I find if I just introduce myself to 3 new people every week, the results seem to take care of themselves!" And they did. He was always over-achieving his new business results, and never failed to make his annual revenue target. Why? Because he focused on doing the activities which drive the results. He understood that you actually couldn't control the result. There are too many factors influencing it: customers, competitors, global economy, terrorism, just to name a few. The only thing you have 100% control over is the type and amount of activity that you do.

Call to action: Take a lesson from the dictionary; you will find ACTIVITY well before you get to RESULT. Implement a process that instills an 'Activity Based Sales Effectiveness' culture throughout the sales team.

2.   Well Defined Marketing Direction with evidence that it is being executed by the Sales-force.

The executive team has a clear idea of the marketing direction, and the company vision. And yet, I consistently find that when talking to the lower ranks, and particularly the front-facing sales people, the water is far murkier! They typically continue to focus on selling the products and services they are comfortable with, despite a different marketing direction espoused by the marketing team. In other words, there is a failure to align the sales efforts, and focus, with the marketing direction formulated to achieve the revenue goals and the overall vision.

Organisations who do this well have taken the time to design a 'Target Market Criteria'. Any decent sales-force automation software or CMS (Customer Management System) has this type of tool you can tailor. In essence, it a simple excel spreadsheet which sorts the wheat from the chaff. It defines the criteria that should exist with a potential client before we would waste our precious time going and talking to them. This tool should contain criteria which are directly linked to the desired marketing direction. It describes the ideal type of client you want given your marketing direction.

Call to action: Have the marketing and sales team jointly build a 'Target Market Criteria' Tool immediately following a presentation on the companies marketing direction. This will create high ownership of doing activity in the field, which will achieve the desired results. Regional Sales Managers then need to be managing and coaching the team to implement activity which matches the criteria, instead of making comfortable 'Latte' calls to existing clients about existing products! Not that would happen in your organisation...would it?

3.   A well developed 'Pipeline' measurement and reporting process.

April. Every year. "Why are we down on budget YTD?" you ask. Back comes the reply, "It's ok, boss, it's in the pipeline!" I love these mysterious pipelines. Magical things. The answer to all budget shortfall in the YTD result. And yet, exactly how much is in this pipeline thingy, will it be enough, and will it land before the 30th of June?

Show me a senior manager who sleeps well at night, and I'll show you a sales organisation which has a uniform way of measuring the volume of opportunities in the pipeline, and an agreed way of assigning it's weighted value. Notice two things in the example Pipeline Prediction Report below in Table One. Firstly, the key figure is the nett value of the pipeline -not the gross value. We should be tracking the nett weighted value because that is the figure, which is likely to land. And secondly, note the agreed weightings, which are dependent on certain events having happened.

Table 1:

Pipeline Prediction Tool		Period:		2004	
Number	**Potential Opportunity**	**Total $'s**	**Weighting**	**Weighted $'s**	
	General Training/speeches				
1	Better Mesh VIC - Sales coachin	12,500	40%	5000	
2	DEWR - ACC project	5,500	90%	4950	
3	Harry's Reinforcing - Selling Skill	40,000	80%	32000	
4	Landmark Investments	20000	60%	12000	
5	Get Online - Asia	100000	20%	20000	
6	Snackaway NAC	20000	80%	16000	
7	Sally's Seeds.	3000	80%	2400	
	Sub-Total:	**201,000**		**92,350**	
	Note:				
	40% = Met with main DCM. Very keen and have the budgets				
	60% = Written proposal/Action Plan submitted				
	80% = Verbal confirmation & dates booked				
	90% = Signed 'Services Agreement' received				

Outcomes achieved by this tool:

Consistent understanding of what a 40%, 60%, or 80% chance means

Simple process to understand if you need to do more activity out in the market place, or whether you are ahead of the game

Regional, national or global forecast report by asking all Regional sales managers to track and report on their pipeline

Ability to predict where you will land

4. Complete a Reverse Planning process to determine the level of activity required to produce the result.

At a recent meeting with an Australasian CEO of a global Australian company, he told me the average conversion ratios of the sales-force, and the required level of activity required to drive results. He had his finger on the pulse because the sales management team had bred a culture of 'Reverse Planning' throughout the organisation. Now, this is not rocket science. In fact, it is so simple, it is profound. Take the desired results target, then, get in reverse. Let's back it up and see what activity levels need to be done in order to guarantee the results. For example, if you want $1m in new business, and the average size of the order is $10k, then math tells you that 100 orders are required. If your team's average ratio of quotes to order is 3 to 1, then you need 300 quotes out there in the market place. If your ratio of appointments, which results in a quote-averages at 2 to 1, then 600 appointments need to be conducted by the sales-force.

Depending on each sales person's skills, abilities and experience, everyone's ratios will be different. But, the law of averages will apply. Benchmarks can be set, and the result will be in the bag, providing the activity levels are completed. Again, over to the regional sales managers to ensure this occurs, because the old well-used doctrine still applies: 'Measure what you want done!'

In conclusion:

Show me an organisation that achieves its revenue targets consistently, and I'll show you a business development team who scores well on the above four areas. The 'Health of your Sales-force' checklist in Table 2 might be a good place to determine your current reality. Of course, if you don't have these four things happening, then fear not.

You can always continue to fall back on the Crystal Ball Method, and then place both hands together, look upwards, and pray that the result happens!

Sleep tight.

Table 2: 'Health of your Sales-force' Checklist

		Yes	No	?
1.	We have an 'Activity Based' culture which focuses on the key activities which will drive results?			
2.	We have incentive and bonus schemes which reward both activities and results?			
3.	We have a well-defined marketing direction?			
4.	Our marketing direction has been clearly communicated to the business development team/sales-force?			
5.	We have developed a 'Target Market Criteria' tool which defines the ideal type of client we want to do business with?			
6.	We have a formalised Pipeline prediction tool which assesses the net probability of each opportunity?			
7.	Our Pipeline probability scores and ranking our uniform and agreed?			
8.	We know our average conversion ratios by individual, team, region and company?			
9.	We have established performance benchmarks for key conversion ratios?			
10.	We have a training and development plan in place which will address skills gaps and give the sales-force the confidence to implement the activities which will drive results?			

Health check:

If you ticked YES to 8-10 of these criteria, relax, you're already enjoying a great night's sleep.

If only 5-7 ticks in the YES column, broken sleep and the odd nightmare will be the norm.

Less than 5 ticks... consult your doctor. Stress medication and sleeping pills will be a must!

RECALL CHART

© Ian Stephens And Enrich Training & Development

To order your colour copies of recall chart and
individual law posters;

Contact us via: **www.ianstephensspeaks.com**
Or e-mail: **support@enrichyourresults.com.au**

Programs and Workshops by enRich Training & Development

SALES PEOPLE TOOLS AND SKILLS

Activate – An Activity-Based Sales Effectiveness Program

A two day workshop which embeds a standard sales methodology within an organisation and creates a framework for ongoing 'Sales Effectiveness Coaching' by Sales Managers. Participants are exposed to the universal laws governing sales effectiveness, then design and create their own suite of company and product specific tools to maximise sales results.

Excelerate - Consultative Selling Skills

A two day program that is tailored to your business and designed to educate your business development people NOT to sell. Instead the aim should be to uncover and demonstrate an understanding of the client's needs and then present an appropriate solution, which solves their issues, challenges and concerns.

Overcoming Objections

A two day program that explores what happens prior to the buyer making the commitment to purchase and how to use a six step process that supports you in recognising, understanding and overcoming the objections raised in a way that avoids conflict.

Influencing the Customer

A two day program that facilitates concluding a current sales opportunity while accelerating the consolidation of the supplier-customer relationship for the long-term, including a voyage of self-discovery for participants and broadening of their understanding of other's personality preferences.

Contact us via: www.ianstephensspeaks.com
Or e-mail: support@enrichyourresults.com.au

SALES MANAGEMENT AND COACHING

Elevate – A Sales Activity Management Program
(Tools & Skills)
A two day workshop which embeds a standard Sales Management methodology within an organisation. Participants learn a combination of skills and tools that can be used to motivate and manage the sales-force. The tools are practical, system based and measurable. They create predictability in the performance of your sales team and, critically, your region, state or national revenue result.

Navigate – A Coaching Mastery Program
A two day Program that embeds a coaching methodology for the leaders and managers of people. Participants learn the soft skills of performance management and a series of tools that can be used to develop and evolve their people according to their individual needs, differences and styles.

> **Contact us via:**   www.ianstephensspeaks.com
> **Or e-mail:**   support@enrichyourresults.com.au

Special Bonus Material

If you would like more information on the strategies, tools and techniques available to help you improve your sales perfor-mance and grow your business register at:

www.ianstephensspeaks.com

ADVANCED SKILLS

Persuasive Communication

This one day program takes skillful salespeople and negotiators to a whole new level of understanding rapport and why people behave in the way they do, particularly under stress or moments of change, then develops the framework to re-package your communication to have more impact where it counts.

Compelling Presentations

Split into a 2 day program and a 1 day workshop so that participants can scrutinise the principles of effective presentations, hear how to maximise their impact and appeal, then tackle the task of adding these skills and processes to their own style of presenting.

Skillful Negotiation

A two day practical and tailored workshop in which participants learn to identify the stages of negotiation and understand the styles of negotiators. Then using a consistent structured process they prepare for, and role play, a real live negotiation which will be taking place in the near future.

Strategic Key Account Management

A two or three day practical workshop that embeds a structured, holistic approach to Strategic Key Account Management that is sales activity driven and easily to implement. During the workshop participants will complete two actual live plans and leave with a process easily replicated for them and their organisation.

Contact us via: **www.ianstephensspeaks.com**
Or e-mail: **support@enrichyourresults.com.au**

www.ingramcontent.com/pod-product-compliance
Lightning Source LLC
Chambersburg PA
CBHW071149200326
41519CB00018B/5170